WHAT THE ELEPHANT WAS

Strange Prehistoric Elephants

Books by Miriam Schlein

Project Panda Watch
What the Elephant Was

Imperial mammoth

WHAT THE ELEPHANT WAS

Strange Prehistoric Elephants

by MIRIAM SCHLEIN

Illustrated with Museum Drawings, Paintings and Photographs

ATHENEUM 1985 NEW YORK

Acknowledgment

I wish to thank Dr. Richard H. Tedford of the Department of Vertebrate Paleontology at the American Museum of Natural History, New York City, for his careful reading of the penultimate version of this manuscript, and for his expert counsel during our several consultations.

Library of Congress Cataloging in Publication Data

Schlein, Miriam.
   What the elephant was.

   SUMMARY: Discusses how the elephant developed from a small, pig-like animal into the large, trunked and tusked creature of today.
   1. Elephants, Fossil—Juvenile literature.
[1. Elephants. 2. Elephants, Fossil. 3. Prehistoric animals] I. Title.
QE882.P8S35   1985   569′.6   85-7415
ISBN 0-689-31166-4

Copyright © 1985 by Miriam Schlein
All rights reserved
Published simultaneously in Canada by
   Collier Macmillan Canada, Inc.
Composition by P&M Typesetting, Inc.
   Waterbury, Connecticut
Printed and bound by Maple-Vail, Binghamton, New York
   Binghamton, New York
Designed by Marilyn Marcus
First Edition

Picture Credits

American Museum of Natural History, frontis, ii, 2, 4, 9, 10, 15, 16, 18–19, 20, 21, 22, 23, 31, 33, 49, 60
Miriam Schlein 5, 27, 32, 46, 52, 53, 54
Field Museum of Natural History 6, 42–43
American Philosophical Society 35
The Smithsonian Institution 38–39, 40, 51
Roy Pinney 56
U.S. Fish and Wildlife Service 58

Map and chart by Elizabeth Weiss 13, 24–25

Contents

    Time Chart   1
1. **A Strange Discovery**   3
2. **The New Pre-Elephants Wander**   11
3. **Shovel-Tuskers, Hoe-Tuskers and Mastodons**   14
    Chart: What the Elephant Was   24
4. **How the Elephant Got Its Trunk**   26
5. **The First "True Elephants" Appear**   30
6. **Giant and Dwarf Elephants**   36
7. **Woolly Mammoths of the Ice Age**   38
8. **The Giants Disappear**   47
9. **Today's Elephants**   50
10. **Present-day Relatives of the Elephant**   57
    Author's Note   60
    Glossary   61
    Bibliography   63
    Index   64

TIME CHART

Epoch	When	Some Changes on Earth	Proboscidean Development
HOLOCENE (Recent times)	Began about 10,000 years ago. We are still in Holocene.	It is warmer once again. The glaciers have retreated. Man lives all over the earth.	Woolly mammoth, mastodon and practically all other proboscideans have become extinct. Only African and Asiatic (Indian) elephants survive.
PLEISTOCENE	From 2 million years ago to about 10,000 years ago.	It is the Ice Age. Often, large parts of the earth are covered with sheets of thick ice. There are warmer, in-between periods called interglacials.	Many proboscideans and other animals move southward to escape the cold and find food. Others, like the woolly mammoth, adapt to the cold.
PLIOCENE	From 5 million years ago to 2 million years ago.	The world becomes colder. Rockies and other mountain ranges rise higher. There are still many volcanic eruptions.	Many new forms of "true elephants" develop, including large forest elephants, mammoths and *Stegodon*. Many older forms—Deinotheres, mastodons, gomphotheres and others—are also still in existence.
MIOCENE	From 25 million years ago to 5 million years ago.	For the first time, Africa is connected to other parts of the earth by land bridges.	*Moeritherium, Palaeomastodon* and *Phiomia* are now extinct. New forms—Deinotheres (hoe-tuskers), mastodons and the long-jawed gomphotheres—develop. Many wander out of Africa into Europe, Asia and later into North America. The first primitive "true elephant" *Stegotetrabelodon* appears toward the end of this time.
OLIGOCENE	From 36 million years ago to 25 million years ago.	The Tethys Sea becomes smaller. There is more land and less water covering the earth. Alps and Himalaya Mountains begin to rise. There are many volcanic eruptions.	*Moeritherium, Palaeomastodon* and *Phiomia* still live on in Africa.
EOCENE	From 55 million years ago to 36 million years ago.	Much of earth is warmer, more tropical than now. More of it is covered by water.	Piglike *Moeritherium* in African swamps. *Palaeomastodon* and *Phiomia* in woodlands and forests.

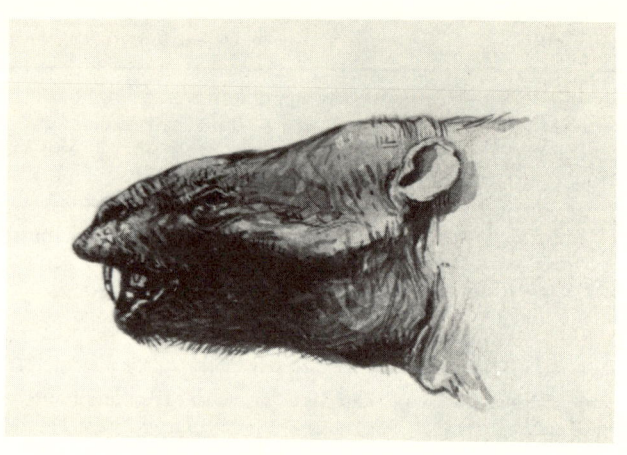 

Head of the *Moeritherium* (above) compared with head of present-day elephant (right)

Moeritherium

1 A Strange Discovery

The men searching in the desert shouted with excitement. They were in Egypt, hunting for fossils—bones of animals that had lived millions of years ago.

They had already made many interesting finds: bones of giant tortoises, whales and sea cows that had been buried here, covered by the desert sand for many millions of years.

But what they just found excited them even more. They had found bones—and now the skull and teeth—of the earliest relative of the elephant ever to be discovered.

What did this early elephant relative look like? Certainly not like an elephant. In fact, it looked more like a big pig. It had no trunk. It was about two feet high (around 60 centimeters), with short legs and a body about eight feet long (around 2½ meters). It had a long head and snout, and its eyes and ears were high on the head, like those of a hippo.

The men who made the discovery were two Englishmen, Charles Andrews and Hugh Beadnell. They had been sent on the expedition by the British Museum of Natural History. What made them think this piglike animal had anything to do with the elephant? Even though it did not *look* like an elephant, it seemed to have some definite elephantlike qualities.

4 What the Elephant Was

The most important of these qualities was its teeth. The molars, or "cheek teeth," resembled those of other prehistoric animals related to the elephant. (Ones that had lived at a later time, but whose fossils had already been discovered.) Also, the incisors—the front "cutting teeth"—were curved and long. Though they were not really tusks as we think of them, it seemed likely that these long, curved teeth might have been the early beginnings of what, in later elephants, developed into tusks. (Elephant tusks are teeth that keep on growing.)

Skull and teeth of *Moeritherium*

Elephants have very long thigh bones and short, rounded feet

The ancient whale, Basilosaurus

Elephant legs and feet are also unusual. Unlike most other animals, their thigh bone is long in proportion to the rest of the leg. Their feet are short and rounded. We know now that the feet and leg bones of this ancient animal, although smaller, were formed in a similar way.

The place in Egypt where Beadnell and Andrews made their discovery is known as the Fayum area, not far from the city of Cairo. There is a lake there that used to be called Lake Moeris. So, they named this early elephant relative *Moeritherium*, after the place where it was found. (The suffix -therium means "beast.") *Moeritherium* lived in Africa between 55 and 36 million years ago during the time called the *Eocene*. (See time chart)

Today, most of northern Africa is desert. But during the Eocene much of that area was covered by a huge sea which we call the Tethys Sea. Here, giant sharks and sea turtles swam, as well as sharp-toothed 60-foot-long ancient whales called *Basilosaurus*. It was in the swamps at the edge of the Tethys that *Moeritherium* lived, wading about, eating roots and water plants.

Beadnell and Andrews had chosen to search in the Fayum area for a special reason. The slopes and cliffs around the lake were made up of exposed layers or "strata" of earth millions of years old. It was a perfect place to find fossils.

Searching further, they soon discovered two more forms of early relatives of the elephant. One they named *Phiomia* (meaning "one who lives in the lake region"). *Phiomia* had long teeth resembling short tusks growing from its upper jaw. It also had wide flat teeth extending from the lower jaw. *Phiomia* was somewhat larger than *Moeritherium*: about four feet high (around 125 centimeters). It lived in wooded areas, where it grazed on grass and other vegetation.

The other form they named *Palaeomastodon* ("ancient mastodon"). *Palaeomastodon* stood about five feet high (about 150 centimeters), and had short upper and lower incisor "tusks." But the most important thing was this; both animals had an extra-long upper lip—so long that it hung down a bit over the lower jaw. This was probably the first sign of what was later to become the elephant's trunk.

Since *Paleomastodon* was a larger animal, its upper lip might have been a bit longer than *Phiomia*'s. We don't know.

Palaeomastodon lived in the forests. Like *Phiomia*, it ate grass. Very likely it also used that long upper lip to grasp branches and pull down leaves to eat.

We cannot really call these animals "elephants." A good name for them might be "pre-elephants."

How can we know so much about these ancient pre-elephants, which no one has ever seen alive? The fossil remains give us some very good clues.

The way foot bones are formed tells how an animal stood, walked and ran. The way the nasal bones of the skull are formed can give us some idea whether the animal had a trunk. The high placement of *Moeritherium*'s eyes and ears is a good indication that it was amphibious like the hippo and spent a lot of time in water.

From fossil leaves and flower pollen we can learn what kind of plants and trees grew in the area and this, in turn, tells us what the climate was at that time. (We know that fig trees and ferns, for example, grow in warm places.) The shape of fossilized dunes can even tell us in which direction the prevailing winds blew in a certain area millions of years ago.

By analyzing the amount of the element strontium found in fossil bones we can learn what an animal ate. (More strontium becomes concentrated in bones of an animal that eats leaves, less if it eats grass, even less if it eats meat.) And so each fossil bone and tooth puts into place another piece of the puzzle of what these animals of the past looked like, and how they lived.

We can tell *when* an animal lived by the stratum or level of earth in which it is found. Geologists can date layers by the kinds of soil or sediment that formed them. A stratum (layer) is known to be older if it has fewer remains of species that still exist; a more recent stratum has a higher percentage of remains of still-existing species.

The *Phiomia* and *Palaeomastodon* fossils found by Beadnell and Andrews were in earth layers dating from the time we call the Oligocene (36 to 25 million years ago). So, for many years, scientists thought that this was

This is what we think *Moeritherium* (bottom), *Phiomia* (upper right) and *Palaeomastodon* (upper left) may have looked like.

the time when these animals first appeared on earth. Then, in the 1960s, additional remains of *Phiomia* and *Palaeomastodon* were found in even earlier layers from the Eocene era. So we know now that they also existed during that earlier time, along with *Moeritherium*.

All three of these animals probably descended from some even earlier common ancestor. (See chart on p. 24)

Beadnell and Andrews made their discoveries between 1901 and 1904. These, as well as important fossil discoveries made soon after by Henry Fairfield Osborn, an American who led a group from the American Museum of Natural History, were the beginning of the strange story of what the elephant was, long ago, and how it got to be the animal we know today.

Phiomia

2 The New Pre-Elephants Wander

In Eocene and Oligocene times, the earth was different from the way it is now. There was more water and less land. Much of Colorado, Utah, and Wyoming was under a large lake. Florida was under the sea. Many mountain ranges were not yet formed. It was warmer then; more parts of the earth were hot, moist and tropical.

But, as millions of years passed, the face of the earth slowly changed. Many active volcanoes pushed material up from the earth. Inner earth movements and the cracking of the earth's crust also pushed upward to form new mountain ranges, like the Rockies, where there had once been just flat land.

As the land built up, many areas that were once under water became dry land. This caused another change. Because land does not hold heat as well as water, the climate of the entire earth gradually got cooler, although it was still warmer than it is now.

As the earth changed in these ways, the animals changed as well. Slowly, new types of animals developed from the old. *Moeritherium, Phiomia,* and *Palaeomastodon* died out, and new forms of pre-elephants developed—ones better able to survive in this new drier and cooler world.

Earlier, Africa had been surrounded by water. But now, for the first time, there were land connections linking Africa with other parts of the world.

A narrow land bridge built up across the Mediterranean Sea, linking Africa to Spain. Because of land build-up, northeast Africa also now touched Asia. Africa was no longer an isolated continent. And so, for the first time, African animals were able to wander to other parts of the world.

It was at this time that the newer types of ancient pre-elephants first left the African continent. Their descendents, of many strange and different types, ultimately reached almost every part of the world. With the exception of a few places impossible for them to reach, such as Australia, Antarctica, and scattered oceanic islands, they literally wandered over the earth.

Early pre-elephants wandered from their original home in Africa. Their later descendents reached almost every part of the world. The arrows on this map show the general direction and extent of their travels.

Dotted parts of the map show the smaller range of present-day elephants.

African elephants: parts of Africa south of the Sahara Desert.
Asiatic (Indian) elephants: parts of India; Sri Lanka (formerly called Ceylon); Bhutan; Bangladesh, Nepal, Burma, Thailand, Malaysia, Laos, Vietnam, Democratic Kampuchia (formerly called Cambodia) and the Yunnan province of southern China.

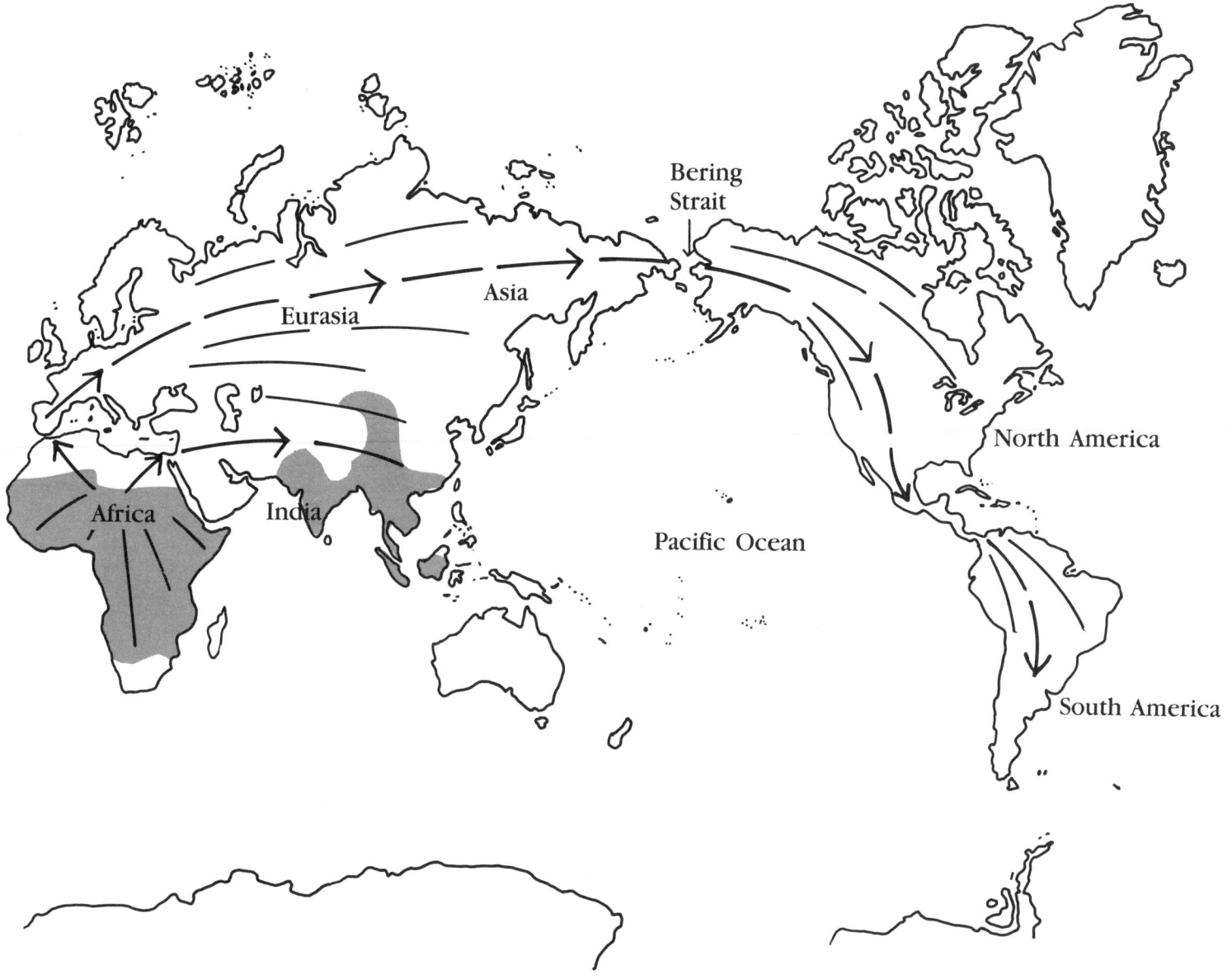

3 Shovel-Tuskers, Hoe-Tuskers and Mastodons

> *Proboscidea* (pruh-bus-*sid*-ee-uh) is the scientific name for today's elephants and all of their early prehistoric relatives. It comes from the word proboscis (pruh-*bos*-sis), meaning long snout or trunk.

Deinotherium (meaning "terrible beast") was one of the first proboscidean wanderers. Some wandered north over the new land bridge into Europe. Others went east into Asia. Early deinotheres were about 8 feet high (2½ meters), with a short trunk, and short, curved tusks in the lower jaw. Because the tusks were shaped something like a garden hoe, growing downward, then curving back toward the body, deinotheres are sometimes called "hoe-tuskers."

Tusks are often used by an animal to defend itself. But a hoe-tusker's tusks could not be used this way because they curved in toward its own body. When the first hoe-tusker fossils were found, scientists could not figure out how the animal used the tusks. Some thought that perhaps hoe-tuskers lived in the water and used their tusks to hook themselves onto the shore while they slept, to keep from drifting away and drowning.

Because the first hoe-tusker fossils that were found lacked foot and leg bones, some scientists thought that instead of feet, hoe-tuskers had flippers like a seal, and when they came up on land, they used the tusks to pull themselves along.

When foot and leg bones were finally found, a simpler theory was developed; hoe-tuskers used their hoe-shaped tusks like a hoe—to dig up food from the ground. But even that does not seem likely. The tusks were very short. To use them for digging, the animal would have been forced to kneel down on its front legs. This would put it in a very dangerous position and make it difficult for it to escape attack.

Hoe-tuskers lived in the forests. It is now thought likely that they used their hoe-shaped tusks to rip edible bark from tree trunks.

Some scientists think that the hoe-tuskers,

Deinotherium (dine-uh-*theer*-ee-yum) was sometimes called the "hoe-tusker."

16 What the Elephant Was

or deinotheres, may be descended from *Moeritherium*. Others think not; they feel that each developed independently, but that both are descended from some earlier common ancestor.

Hoe-tuskers existed on earth for almost 25 million years. In all that time, their basic form changed very little; they simply kept getting larger. The last of the hoe-tuskers stood about 13 feet (4 meters) at the shoulder. It is unusual for an animal to exist so long on earth and to change so little in ways other than size. In the end, though, about one million years ago, the line of deinotheres died out. They are not the ancestors of our present-day elephants.

Mastodons, which lived about the same time, were quite large, some standing 10 feet (3 meters) tall, with long tusks curving from their upper jaw, sometimes reaching 9 feet (3½ meters) in length.

Mastodons had good-sized trunks and were in many ways elephantlike in appearance. Yet in some ways they were different. Many mastodons had four tusks—two in the upper jaw and two in the lower jaw. (Today's elephants have only upper tusks.) Mastodons' bodies were longer than those of today's elephant. And their lower jaw—especially in early mastodons—was much longer than that of today's elephant. (Elephants today have a very short, downturned lower jaw.)

While the hoe-tuskers spread through Europe and Asia, the mastodons wandered even farther. From Asia, they crossed a land bridge, which existed then over the Bering Strait, and entered North America. Fossil mastodon remains have been found in most parts of the continent.

A complete skeleton was found in 1845 by Dr. John Warren near Newburgh, New York. Named the "Warren Mastodon," it was mounted and can be seen now at the American Museum of Natural History in New York City.

Many mastodons were elephantlike in appearance. This painting is based on the skeletal reconstruction of the famous "Warren Mastodon" found in New York State.

Remains of more than one hundred American mastodons were found at Big Bone Lick, Kentucky. Here, long ago, there was a lake that became choked with weeds and turned into a thick black bog. Any heavy animal that came close became stuck and sank to its death. Along with the mastodon fossils were remains of bison, moose and horses.

The Rancho La Brea Tar Pits is another such place where many mastodons, saber-toothed tigers, camels, giant wolves, and many other animals became trapped. You can see their fossils at the site of the pit, located in Los Angeles, California. There are also La Brea fossils at the American Museum of Natural History in New York.

There are American Indian legends that speak of huge animals "with long noses." These were probably mastodons, which roamed North America until about 8,000 years ago.

Many kinds of animals became trapped in the La Brea Tar Pits.

Gomphotheres (gom-*foh*-theers) are often called long-jawed mastodons.

Shovel-Tuskers, Hoe-Tuskers and Mastodons

As the mastodons wandered through the world, living in different environments, they developed many different forms.

One was the large special group known as *gomphotheres*. What sets the gomphotheres apart from the other mastodons is a slight difference in their tooth formation. But, because many gomphotheres (though not all of them) had especially long lower jaws, they are often called *long-jawed mastodons*. The other mastodons are sometimes called *true mastodons*.

Some of the long-jawed mastodons had still another name—*shovel-tuskers*. You can see why.

Platybelodon ("flat-toothed one") was a shovel-tusker whose lower jaw was so long and wide it looked like a trough. Its short, wide flat lower tusks, growing side by side, stuck straight out to form the "shovel," which it used to scoop up plants and roots to eat. *Platybelodon* lived in Asia.

The similar-looking *Torynobelodon* ("spoon-tusked one") lived in North America.

Amebelodon was a shovel-tusker that lived in Europe, Asia, and in areas of North America from Florida to the West Coast. The total combined length of its lower jaw and tusks was 6 feet (almost 2 meters). Its upper lip was long enough to reach the front tip of the tusks and hang over a bit. *Amebelodon* used its shovel tusks to dig up water plants.

Not all gomphotheres had shovel tusks. *Gnathabelodon*—a "spoon-billed gomphothere"—had no lower tusks. It used the lower jaw itself, which was long and thin-edged, to scoop up its food. *Gnathabelodon* lived in North America.

Amebelodon used its "shovel" tusks to dig up water plants.

Remains of this straight-tusked gomphothere *Anancus* were found in Italy.

Rhynchotherium ("beak-jawed beast") had a long lower jaw that curved downward, like a beak. These gomphotheres lived in Africa, Asia, and North America.

Anancus was a gomphothere that did not have a long lower jaw. What was special about *Anancus* was its huge upper tusks. They were 10 feet long (about 3 meters) and pointed straight ahead. They were almost as long as the entire rest of the animal. *Anancus* lived in Europe and Asia.

Cordillerion also had special tusks. They were spiral-twisted, like the tusks of a narwhal. *Cordillerion* lived in North America; its remains have been found in Arizona and California. In later times, *Cordillerions* made their way into South America, where they lived on the flat grassy plains, or pampas, as well as high in the Andes Mountains.

The gomphotheres were descended from *Phiomia*. The "true mastodons" were descended from *Palaeomastodon*. Earlier still, they were all descended from some as yet unknown common mastodon ancestor. But the gomphotheres, quite early, branched off to become a very specialized form.

Today's elephants may seem to *look* more like the deinotheres and the "true" mastodons. But they are not descended from them. Today's elephants are more closely related to the gomphotheres—the long-jawed mastodons. (See chart on p. 24)

The spiral-tusked *Cordillerion* was found in the Andes Mountains in Bolivia.

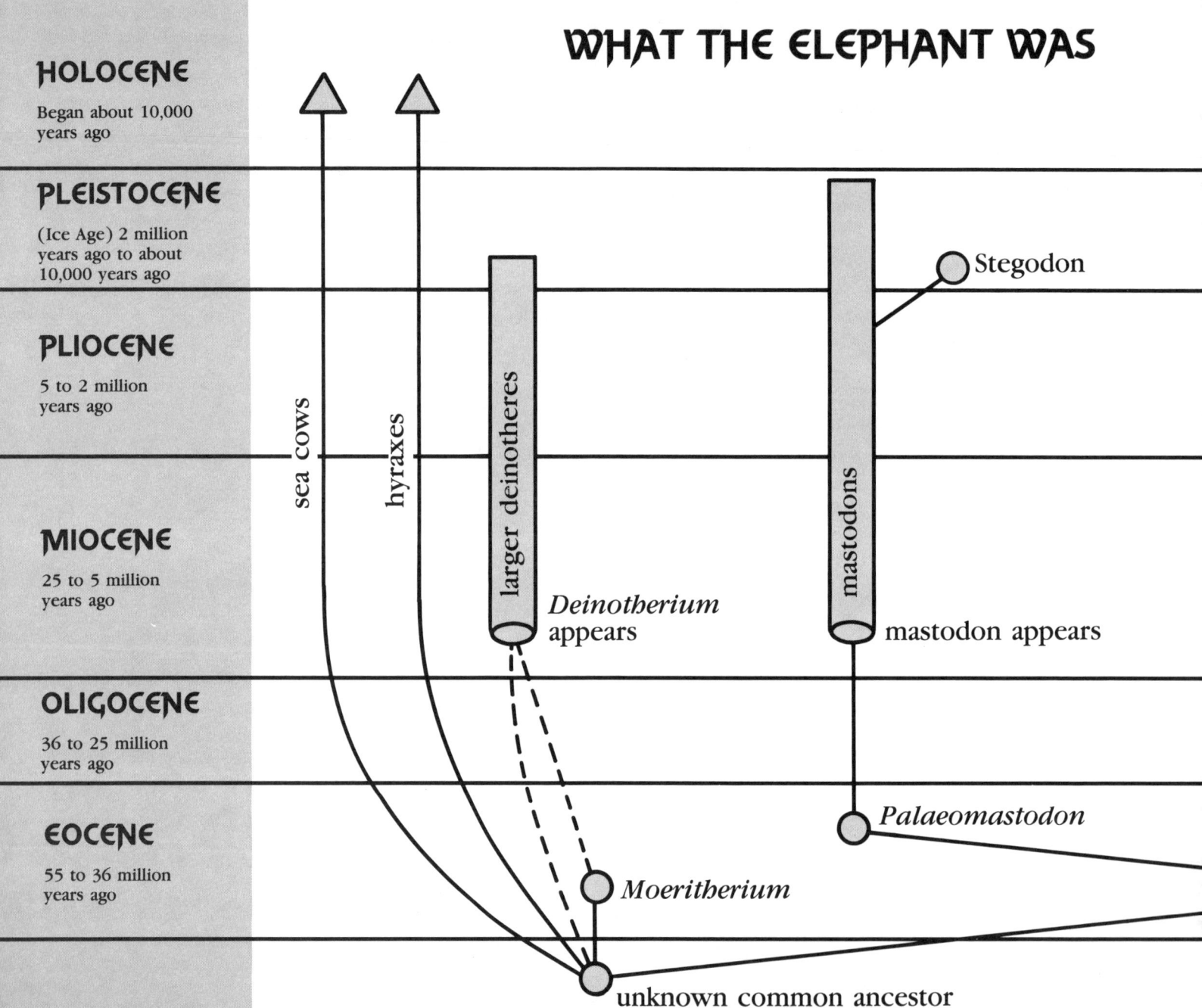

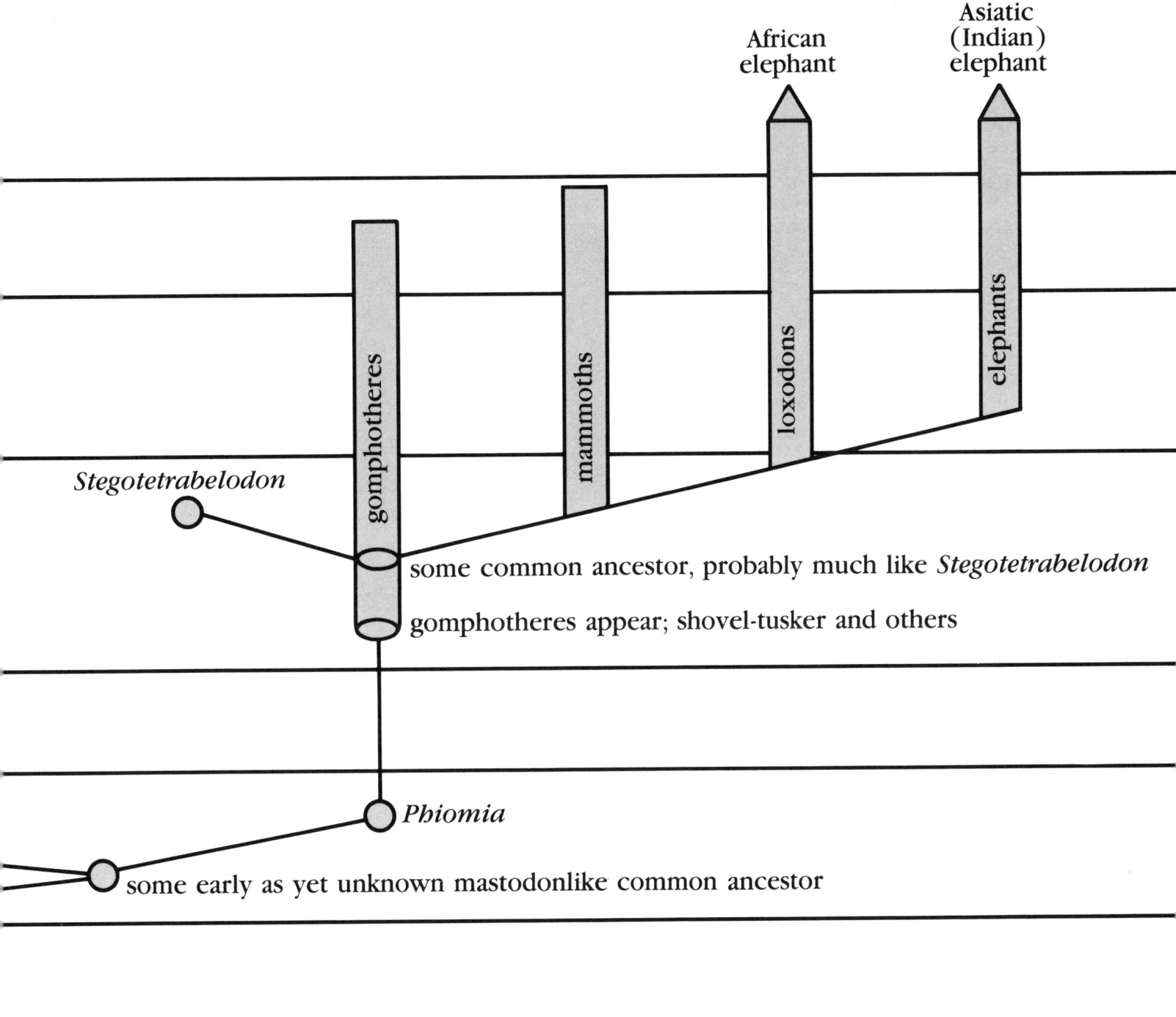

4 How the Elephant Got Its Trunk

> In the High and Far-Off Times, the Elephant...
> had no trunk. He had only a blackish, bulgy nose,
> as big as a boot, that he could wriggle about from side
> to side; but he couldn't pick up things with it ...
>
> —From "The Elephant's Child"
> in *Just So Stories* by Rudyard Kipling

Have you ever wondered how the elephant got its trunk? We were only able to learn the answer to this question when we began finding fossil remains of mastodons and gomphotheres.

Mastodons and gomphotheres were larger than earlier proboscideans. Their heads were higher from the ground—which would make it difficult for them to reach the ground for food and water. Sometimes this sort of problem is solved in nature by having the animal develop a longer neck as it gets larger. But in the case of the pre-elephants that solution by nature would not have worked. Mastodon and gomphothere heads were too heavy to be supported by a long neck. So, the mastodons and gomphotheres developed in a different way. As their height and size increased, they

Have you ever wondered how the elephant got its trunk?

developed longer and longer lower jaws, which enabled them to reach the ground for food and water. As their long lower jaw developed, they developed a long upper lip to match. Then, that long upper lip got to be useful in itself for pulling and grasping things. It was also good for reaching *up* as well as down. In time, it took over the job of food gathering.

The long lower jaw was no longer used for scooping and shoveling, and over time, it got shorter and lost its tusks. But the useful long upper lip remained. Since it now no longer had that long lower jaw to rest on, it just hung down free. In time, the long upper lip changed in form and became a trunk—which is really a combination upper lip and nose. And that is how the elephant got its trunk.

How can an animal change this way? How can a type of animal get bigger, or develop a trunk, or a long jaw?

It happens by something we call *natural selection*. This is how it works.

All people are not alike. Some are taller than others. Some are thinner. Some happen to have shorter fingers ... or bigger feet. In the same way, each individual animal of a certain species is not exactly alike. And just a small difference between two animals might enable one to survive when the other might die. Just a small difference—being a bit bigger, or having a slightly longer jaw, or slightly bigger tusks, for example—might help an individual animal in getting enough food or in escaping its enemies. This special advantage gives it a better chance to survive, to breed, and give birth to young. It is likely that these young would inherit the helpful characteristic, which would again help *them* to survive and breed and have still more young.

In time, there would get to be more and more individuals with this helpful special advantage, because the ones without it would be more apt to die. Finally, *all* the individuals in the species have the advantage. It is no longer anything different or special. The entire species has changed a bit. It takes many, many generations for even a small change to occur throughout a species by natural selection.

Another way a species can change is by *mutation*. An individual animal inherits its qualities from its parents through the makeup of the genes within its cells when it is born. Once in a great while—and it is very rare—an animal is born with a different sort of genetic make-up, which causes the animal to be different. Often, it is what we would call a "freak"—for example, a lamb with three legs. An animal like that generally dies. But sometimes the gene change—or mutation—causes an animal to be different in a useful way, say with a slightly different type of hoof, which may help it to run faster. As a faster runner, this animal has a better chance to survive. Its young inherit the difference and in turn pass it on to their young. We call an animal like this a *sport* or *mutant*. Change by mutation occurs faster throughout a species than change by natural selection.

This is how the proboscideans changed, as millions of years passed. It's the way they got larger. It's the way their incisor teeth became longer and finally developed into tusks. It's the way they developed the superlong lower jaw—which led, in turn, to their most distinctive feature of all—their trunk.

This process of slow change is called evolution.

5 The First "True Elephants" Appear

Many mastodons looked much like elephants. Still, scientists do not consider them "true elephants." Why not? It's because of the kind of teeth they had.

The name *mastodon* was made up by the French naturalist, Baron Georges Cuvier. When Cuvier examined fossil mastodon teeth, he saw they had pairs of raised cusps on them, with "valleys" between each pair. The paired cusps reminded him of female breasts. So he decided mastodon ("breast-toothed" in Latin) was a perfect name for the animal.

Gomphothere teeth also had paired cusps, but in addition, they had smaller cones in the "valleys."

Elephant teeth are quite different. An elephant tooth is made up of many thin vertical bands of dentine, covered by enamel. These bands—called plates—are pressed close and glued together by a bonelike material called cementum. The top chewing edge of the tooth is thus made up of many rough ridges of enamel, dentine and cementum.

If you could look into an elephant's mouth, you would see that the elephant has only one, or at most two, teeth in each jaw. Each tooth is very large. It weighs about 8 pounds (3½ kilograms) and is about a foot (30 centimeters) long. After a tooth has been used for a number of years, it becomes worn

The First "True Elephants" Appear

down and useless. Then a new tooth, one that has been forming in the back of the jaw, moves forward, pushing out the old tooth, which falls out in pieces. The new tooth takes its place.

Each new tooth is bigger and has more ridges than the one before. But an elephant doesn't keep getting new teeth forever. When the sixth set of teeth is worn out, no more teeth develop. The old elephant can't chew its food anymore and will soon die of starvation.

Tusks are teeth, too. They are superlong incisors. They do not fall out. In fact, tusks keep growing all through an elephant's lifetime. So they are a good indication of age. The longer the tusks, the older the elephant.

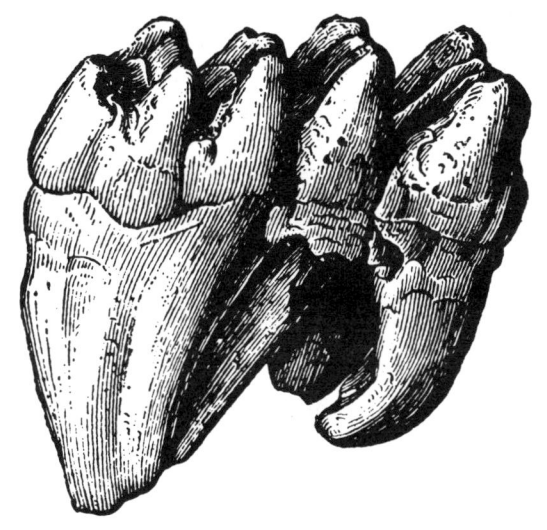

Mastodon teeth had raised cusps.

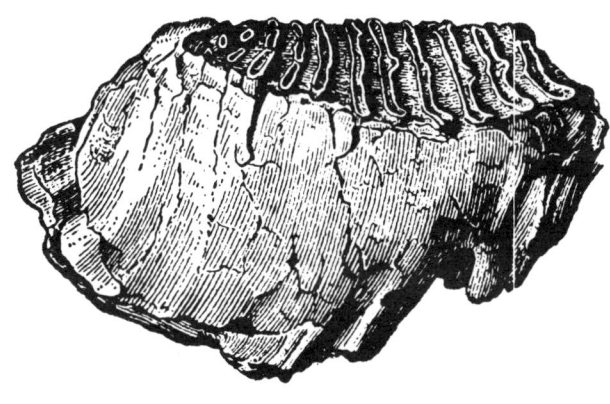

Elephant teeth have ridges.

Elephant skull and teeth. An elephant tooth weighs about 8 pounds and is about 12 inches long. Here you can see the beginnings of the new teeth, pushing forward.

The First "True Elephants" Appear

About two million years ago, a new kind of proboscidean appeared in Asia, one called *Stegodon*. The male *Stegodon*'s tusks grew so close together there was no space for his trunk to hang between them, so his trunk had to hang off to the side. But the most important thing about *Stegodon* was not its tusks, but its teeth.

Stegodon seemed to be the earliest proboscidean found to have a primitive kind of ridged teeth that somewhat resembled those of a modern elephant. They were not as high. And there were not as many ridges. Still, *Stegodon*'s teeth were definitely different from the cusps and crests of mastodons and gomphotheres.

Stegodon ("roof-toothed one") was discovered in the late 1800s. And, for many years, because of its teeth, it was considered the first "true elephant."

The male *Stegodon*'s trunk had to hang off to the side.

Then, in the 1960s, a startling new fossil discovery was made in Africa—of a proboscidean that lived seven million years ago, during the Miocene (a good bit farther back in the past than *Stegodon*) that also had ridged, elephant-like teeth. It was given the name *Stegotetrabelodon*.

Stegotetrabelodon teeth had a flattened chewing surface, with 5 to 7 ridges running across them. The tooth moved forward in the jaw and was replaced by a new tooth, in a progressive tooth replacement method like that of the modern elephant. Now, *Stegotetrabelodon*, not *Stegodon*, is considered the first kind of "true elephant."

They were fairly large animals, up to 10 feet in height (about 3 meters) and had the short downturned lower jaw of a modern elephant. A variety of different species of *Stegotetrabelodon* have been found. Some had long, slim tusks 5½ feet long (almost 2 meters); other had much shorter tusks. Some species had both upper and lower tusks. Others, like today's elephants, had tusks in the upper jaw only.

Stegotetrabelodon was a descendant of the gomphotheres. Today's elephants and the *Stegotetrabelodons* probably both descended from some as yet unknown common ancestor. When and if we ever find it, it will probably look much like *Stegotetrabelodon*. This animal was an important link between the past and present. It existed until the early Pliocene, about 4 million years ago.

The First "True Elephants" Appear

Stegotetrabelodon was the first "true elephant."

6 Giant and Dwarf Elephants

It is no accident that this new kind of tooth developed during the Miocene. The world was getting colder. When climate changes, vegetation changes. Different sorts of vegetation began to grow in this colder world. Instead of big-leafed soft tropical plants, there were more tough cold-weather grasses and trees with tougher foliage.

This is where the new true elephants had a real advantage over the mastodons and other pre-elephants. Mastodon-type teeth with cusps were fine for chewing softer tropical vegetation. But the ridged teeth of *Stegotetrabelodon,* with their rough chewing surface, were much better for chewing the tough grasses and twigs now common in this colder world.

More kinds of "true elephants" soon developed. Among these were large forest elephants (*Elephas namadicus*) living in southern Europe and northern Africa. They were 14 feet high (more than 4 meters) and had tremendous long straight tusks. Their skulls were formed in an unusual way, with a strange, crownlike bony crest on top of the head. (Originally, this early elephant was called *Palaeoloxodon* and is still sometimes referred to by this name.)

Dwarf elephants also developed. Dwarf elephants lived on islands—on Santa Rosa Island off the California coast, in the Philippines, and on islands in the Mediterranean. The smallest, *Elephas falconeri,* lived on the island of Malta in the Mediterranean. They were less than three feet high (less than 1 meter).

Why were they so small? The channel between Malta and the mainland was once narrower and shallower. Large elephants probably originally walked out to the island—at least part of the way. When rising seas cut the island off from the mainland, the elephants remained.

There was one good thing about living on the island. There were no predators there—no meat-eaters, like wolves or tigers or cave bears. But one thing was not so good. The supply of vegetation on the island was limited, and elephants, because of their large size, need a lot of food.

When elephants live in an area where there is the danger of attacking predators, large size is an advantage. But here, that no longer held true. In fact, the opposite was true. Because of the limited food supply, large size became a disadvantage. What happened was that individual elephants who were somewhat smaller (thus needing slightly less food) were better able to remain healthy and breed and have young—who, in turn, were also apt to be on the small side.

In this way, as many generations passed, the elephants got to be smaller and smaller by the process of natural selection. It took several hundred thousand years for the dramatic change in size to occur.

For the same reasons, there were also dwarf deer and dwarf hippos on Malta.

Why Was the World Getting Colder?

Mountains had been pushing up higher and higher. On the new high mountain peaks, it was so cold, snow did not melt and remained year after year. This meant less meltwater ran down to the lakes and seas in the spring, which in turn made the lakes and seas smaller. Since land does not retain solar heat as efficiently as water, this loss of water on the earth's surface caused the earth's climate to become colder.

7 Woolly Mammoths of the Ice Age

There were still gomphotheres in North America during Pliocene times.

Now there was a mingling of many old and new types: Along with various kinds of new "true elephants," large and small, many pre-elephants also survived. The old deinothere "hoe-tuskers" still existed in the forests of Africa. There were the spiral-tusked *Cordillerions* and other gomphotheres on the plains of North and South America. Another form of true elephant had also developed—the mammoth.

When we say *mammoth*, people usually think of the woolly mammoth. The earliest mammoths were very large animals—some 15 feet high (4 meters). But they were not woolly. During the Pliocene times (5 to 2

When we say mammoth, we usually think of the woolly mammoth.

million years ago), there were a great many of them all over Europe, Africa, and Asia. Then, traveling over the Bering Strait land bridge, as other animals had done before them, they finally arrived in North America, where they roamed in great herds over the western plains, over Mexico, and into parts of South America.

But there were bad times ahead.

As mountaintop snow accumulated year after year, it pressed down heavily, forming snow-ice called névé (nay-vay). Then, glacial sheets of ice began to creep down the mountainsides. In time, five million square miles of ice covered a large part of North America. In places, the ice sheet was almost 2 miles thick (3½ kilometers). If you draw a line on a map across Wyoming, Ohio and Pennsylvania, it will show you the southern border of the ice. Ice also covered parts of England, France, Germany, and Scandinavia, as well as northern Asia.

The Ice Age had arrived. It was the time of earth history we call the Pleistocene (2 million years ago to 10,000 years ago).

Many animals moved southward, away from the ice sheet as it came slowly down from the north. Often groups of animals hit dead ends—mountains, or bodies of water they could not cross—as they pushed southward. Since they could neither go back or forward, many perished.

Others were more successful in reaching places where they could survive. Many gomphotheres and mastodons found a narrow strip of land leading south. Pushing through its thick jungles, they found their way to warmer lands in South America.

Some animals did not have to move southward. They were able to adapt quickly to the new harsh conditions and were able to remain and survive in the cold regions. It was at this time that the mammoth developed its woolly coat. Their bodies were covered with fine, soft hair. Over that grew thick, long, coarse reddish-brown fur, which, around the neck and trunk and sides, was 15 inches long (38 centimeters). Under their skin, they also had a 3-inch (7 centimeters) layer of fat.

Woolly mammoths developed special teeth that were a further help in adjusting to the new environment: thick molars with 27 ridges—more ridges than that of a modern elephant. This provided a good surface with

42 What the Elephant Was

which to grind and chew the tough grasses growing on the snow-covered tundra south of the ice sheet.

Woolly mammoth tusks were spectacular, often growing to a length of 16 feet (almost 5 meters), dipping downward, then sweeping up and apart, finally curving back around toward the body. These strangely shaped tusks may have been useful in uncovering snow-covered vegetation. But they could not have been used for self-defense, since they pointed back toward the mammoth's own body.

The woolly mammoths must have been a beautiful sight as they roamed in great herds over the Eurasian and American plains.

The Ice Age was not one long, continuous cold period. At least four times during the Pleistocene the earth warmed up. The ice would melt, new large lakes would be formed by the meltwater, forests and less hardy plants would reappear. Many animals returned to repopulate the old areas, while those that had adapted to the cold—the woolly mammoths,

Woolly mammoths had spectacular tusks.

Woolly Mammoths of the Ice Age

What the Elephant Was

Woolly rhinos

woolly rhinos, musk oxen, caribou and cave bears—wandered farther north.

These warm in-between periods are called *interglacials*. The earth grew warmer than it is now. Animals such as hippos and monkeys lived in England during some interglacials. Then, each time, as the earth turned cold and the ice returned, these animals moved southward once again.

And so, either by moving back and forth, or by adapting to the cold, many animals were able to survive through the Ice Age. But then, toward its end, many kinds of animals—mostly large ones—quite suddenly died out. In fact, so many different kinds of animals died out all over the world that scientists call it a time of "mass extinctions."

Many types of proboscideans had managed to live through practically the entire Ice Age: *Stegodon* in Asia, the long-tusked *Anancus* in Europe, gomphotheres and mastodons in South America, the mammoths and mastodons in North America. But by the end of the Ice Age, practically all of these giants, which had roamed the earth for so long, suddenly disappeared forever.

Why? What happened to them?

Elephants reproduce slowly.

8 The Giants Disappear

Generally, large size is an advantage. For one thing, it helps an animal in self-defense. Usually (but not always), as a type of animal develops, it becomes larger in size. But during the Ice Age, large size became a handicap. During glacial periods, as animals migrated southward away from the cold, animals of all kinds were forced into more limited feeding areas. This must have led at times to fierce competition for food.

Proboscideans need large amounts of food. Normally, they spend 16 hours a day eating to feed those big bodies. One elephant eats 500 pounds (226 kilograms) of food daily. So a limited food supply was a more serious problem for proboscideans than it was for smaller animals.

Also, proboscideans reproduce slowly. A mother elephant is pregnant for almost two years. Often just one young is born at a time, and it is not mature until the age of 8 or 10. A female elephant will bear only 5 or 6 young in her lifetime. In uncertain times, with periodic food shortage, animals that reproduce slowly and have few young do not have as good a chance of survival as animals that give birth more frequently and have large litters.

But these were not the only reason why so many proboscideans and other large animals disappeared from Earth during the Ice Age.

Something else was happening just at this time. A new kind of hunter was spreading over the earth—one that could kill large animals and fast animals and even fierce ones like saber-toothed tigers and cave bears. It was a hunter who could kill proboscideans, too, whose size and tusks had, up until now, always protected them from predators.

The new hunter was Man.

Man had existed before this time. But earlier Man had only rough stone weapons and was not such a skilled hunter. Now men had invented better weapons, like spears and sling shots, which they learned to use with skill. And they did not have to get up close to kill. Using their weapons, they would kill from a distance. No other predator was able to do that.

Man also thought up new ways to kill. They would dig a pit and cover it with branches to conceal it. When a mammoth or mastodon fell into it, it was trapped. From the edge of the pit, men would kill it with spears.

They learned to frighten and stampede a whole herd of horses or mammoths so that they would run over a cliff. The fallen, injured animals were then easy to kill.

In those ways, Man could kill animals bigger, stronger, fiercer and faster than himself. Never before had there been a predator like this.

Men also had fire. And with it, they invented another way to hunt. It is called "fire-driving." They set entire grasslands and forests on fire. The animals were driven out of hiding and more could be killed than would ever be used. And, in setting these fires, Man also destroyed more than the animals killed at the time. They destroyed the habitat—the living space—of generations of animals for many years to come.

In Europe, hippos, woolly rhinos, straight-tusked Anancus, cave bears—animals who had all survived harsh glacial times either by migration or by adaptation—disappeared from the scene.

In North America, as the Ice Age was ending, mastodons and mammoths still roamed the woodlands and forests. There were also many other large animals such as 20-foot (6 meters) ground sloths, heavier than elephants. There were long-nosed peccaries, 4-horned antelopes, 7-foot-long (about 2 meters) armadillos, giant beavers big as bears.

Giant ground sloths and huge armadillos at the end of the Ice Age.

There were camels and horses in America at that time. Then, within a period of about two thousand years, they all became extinct on this continent.

Humans hunted many kinds of animals. But the woolly mammoth was particularly valuable to them. The meat from one mammoth could feed a group of people for a long time. People could also make tents and clothing out of its fur, and tools and daggers out of its tusks.

As far as we know, the woolly mammoth became extinct about ten thousand years ago. Small groups of other proboscideans may still have existed here and there after that time, but so far there is no evidence of this.

9 Today's Elephants

Fossils of more than 350 different species of proboscideans have been found. Probably more exist that we haven't yet discovered. Now, only two species are left: the African elephant (*Loxodonta africana*) and the Asiatic or Indian (*Elephas maximus*).

How are they different from their ancestors?

The head of today's elephant is higher, more domelike, than the longer head of earlier proboscideans. This large head is not as heavy as it would seem because of a system of air spaces within the skull.

A modern elephant's jaw is now very short—nothing like the jaws of the gomphotheres. It has two tusks in the upper jaw only. (Many ancient types had four tusks.) Elephants' ridged teeth have become progressively taller; they are now four times higher than those of early primitive elephants.

Today's elephants are taller than many early proboscideans, but they are not the largest ever. They are smaller than some, like *Elephas namadicus*, the 14-foot high (4 meters) forest elephants of a million years ago.

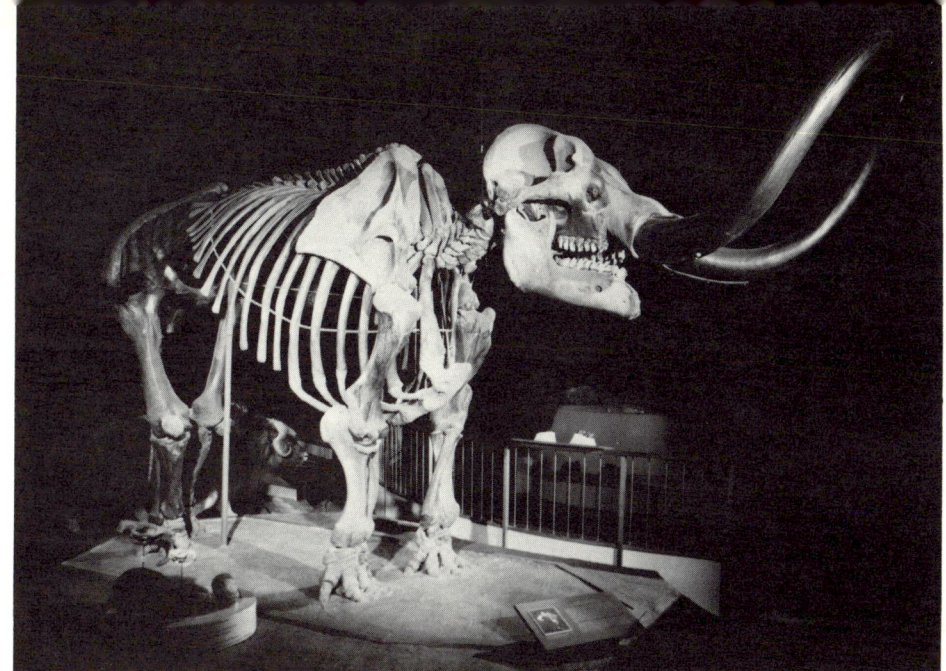

It is interesting to compare the skeletons of the mastodon (to the left) and the mammoth—a more modern form of "true elephant"—below.

You can easily see some differences. The head of the mammoth is high and domed, the jaw of the mastodon is longer. Their body structures are quite different.

The African elephant has very large ears.

Seeing today's two species together, you would have no trouble telling them apart. The most obvious difference is the ears. The African elephant has much larger ears, which are sometimes four feet wide (more than a meter).

The African elephant is generally larger than the Asiatic. A male African elephant can be 11 feet high at the shoulder (more than 3 meters) and weigh 13,000 pounds (almost 6,000 kilograms) with 7-foot tusks (about 2 meters). The female weighs about 9,000 pounds (about 4,000 kilograms) and has more slender tusks. (You may not get a true idea of tusk size at the zoo. Tusks of zoo elephants are often trimmed. Remember also that about 20 percent of the tusk length is hidden in the jaw.)

There is a special variety of African elephant that stands only 7 feet high (about 2 meters). These live in dense forests rather than on the savannah and in river valleys as the larger "bush" elephants do. Although smaller, they are not pygmy elephants.

A male Asiatic elephant (often called the Indian elephant) stands 9 or 10 feet high (about 3 meters) and weighs perhaps 10,000 pounds (about 4,500 kilograms), with tusks around 5 feet long (about 1½ meters). The female Indian elephant often has no tusks at all. If she does have them, they are very short.

The teeth of the Asiatic elephant have more ridges (up to 24) than those of the African elephant (up to 10). The ridges on the teeth of the African elephant are higher and thicker in the center of the tooth, giving a slope to the surface, explaining its name *Loxodonta africana* (slanting-toothed African).

The Asiatic elephant has smaller ears.

If you look closely at their trunks, you will see another difference: the African elephant has two "fingers" at the end of its trunk; the Asiatic has one.

Elephants are social, cooperative animals, living in large herds often led by a mature female. Small groups may sometimes separate from the main herd for a while, but when they join up once again, individuals recognize and greet one another by rubbing cheeks, or entwining trunks. Often, elephants try to support and help a herd member who has been wounded or who is ill.

Elephants are herbivorous, eating vegetation of all sorts; leaves, fruit, grass—but no meat. A newborn elephant weighs about 200 pounds (90 kilograms) and drinks its mother's milk for three years or more. It may live to be about 70. A male elephant is called a bull, a female a cow, a young elephant is called a calf.

Most elephants in the wild now live in protected wildlife preserves, where animals are not supposed to be harmed. But there are poachers who illegally kill elephants for the high price they can get for the ivory tusks, used to make carvings, knife handles and other objects. Elephant hoofs are sometimes used to make stools or umbrella stands, certainly a sad ending for such a great animal.

The most serious danger to elephants is that their habitat, or living space, is becoming smaller. Elephants need large areas in which to live. But each year, more forests, savannahs and woodlands are being cut down and the land used for farms or grazing land for cattle.

Some day we may find out the reason why our two remaining elephant species were able to survive when none of their relatives could do so. Meanwhile, to most of us, elephants are very special animals. Let's hope they can continue to survive in those parts of the world where they still live.

They are social, cooperative animals.

The hyrax is a close relative of the elephant.

10 Present-Day Relatives of the Elephant

It's not easy to tell by looking at them which animals today are the closest relatives of the elephant. One is the hyrax (sometimes called the cony), a small, furry animal that resembles a guinea pig. Some species live in rocky areas, others live in trees.

The hyrax and the elephant both developed from the same ancestor—some animal that lived more than 50 million years ago. Though they developed in different ways, there are some basic things they still have in common. Though much smaller, the leg and foot bones of hyrax resemble in basic structure that of the elephant. The hyrax also has long, curved upper incisor teeth, which, like elephant tusks, keep growing for the lifetime of the animal.

The hyrax was not always small. Some early ones were as large as a pony. So, at one time, the hyrax and the elephant were much closer in size than they are now. Hyraxes live in Africa and Asia.

The other unlikely present-day relatives of the elephant are two sea mammals—the dugongs (sometimes called sea cows) and manatees. They are about 10 feet in length (3 meters), with flippers instead of forefeet. Like elephant teeth, the dugongs' and manatees' teeth move forward when worn and are re-

Present-Day Relatives of the Elephant

placed by new ones forming in the back of the jaw. The male dugong also has tusks—large upper incisors that continually grow, like the elephant's. The manatee does not have tusks.

In the daytime, dugongs rest in deep water. At night, they come close to shore to eat grass growing in shallow water. Often they pile this up on shore, then eat it all at once. Dugongs live off the coast of east Africa and Australia. Dugongs are probably what sailors saw when they claimed to have seen mermaids.

Manatees—often a bit larger than dugongs—also mostly feed at night on water grass, using their flippers to push it toward their mouths. They are gentle creatures, living off the coast of the southeast United States as well as off South America and Africa. Sometimes people feed them by hand. They are often seen in Florida canals, where unfortunately they are at times accidentally hurt or killed by power boats.

As unlikely as it seems, these two sea mammals and the little hyrax are the closest relatives of the elephant living today.

Manatee mother and calf

Author's Note

In some books you may see dates for the periods of earth history that are different from the ones in this book. Because of new information being gathered all the time, these dates are often revised. Also, not all scientists agree on exact dates for when these time spans or *epochs* began and ended.

The dates used in this book are taken from the Elsevier Geological Time Table edited by F. Zan Eysinga, Elsevier Science Publishing Company, 1978.

Since about 1950, there has been a method for determining age that is more accurate than past methods. It is based on finding out the amount of natural radioactive decay that has occurred in certain minerals by means of measuring the amount of Argon gas that has been trapped there. In this way, we can now pinpoint the age of extremely old fossils and layers of rock formation more precisely than we could before.

In some places, you may see the mastodon called *mastodont*. Both forms are correct. It is also sometimes called *Mammut*.

The gomphothere is sometimes called *trilophodon*. *Elephas namadicus* was formerly known as *paleoloxodon*.

The ancient whale *Basilosaurus* used to be called zeuglodon or zeuglodont. You may see this name for it is used in some books.

The metric equivalents are often rounded out, and therefore approximate.

Glossary

Adaptation: change in a species that enables it to live under new conditions.

Armadillo: a burrowing mammal with a bony armor-like covering over its body.

Breed: to mate and produce young.

Dugong: a sea mammal related to the elephant.

Extinct: extinction: a form of life dying out forever, with no possibility of ever reappearing on earth.

Fossil: the preserved remains of an animal or plant from the past, or the imprint of it on stone or some other substance.

Gene: the part of a cell that determines the qualities one inherits from one's parents.

Glacial (from glacier): referring to a large sheet of slowly moving ice.

Habitat: the kind of area in which a certain animal or plant lives.

Herbivorous: referring to animals that eat only plant life and no meat.

Hyrax: a mammal related to the elephant. The present-day hyrax resembles a guinea pig.

Inherit: to have a quality passed down to an individual from its parents.

Manatee: a sea mammal related to the elephant.

Mastodon: a form of early proboscidean generally having teeth with paired, raised cusps that were different from the teeth of modern elephants.

Migration: moving on from one area to another.

Mutant: an individual that is different from others of its species because of a gene change, or mutation.

Glossary

Natural selection: the natural process which makes it possible for animals to change characteristics.

Orders: one of the 19 (or more) large groupings into which all forms of animal and plant life are divided. (For example, all whales, dolphins and porpoises are in the order *Cetacea* (suh-*tay*-shuh); all hoofed mammals having an even number of toes on each foot are in the order Artiodactyla (art-tee-oh-*dack*-till-uh). Not all zoologists agree completely as to how the various animals should be grouped.

Paleontologist: a scientist who learns about forms of prehistoric life by studying fossil remains.

Pampas: grass-covered plain or prairie of South America.

Poacher: someone who hunts illegally.

Predator: a meat-eater who hunts and kills other animals to eat.

Proboscidea: the order or grouping of animal life that includes all elephants and related forms of pre-elephants of the past.

Savannah: a broad, flat open plain.

Shovel-tusker: any one of a number of long-jawed mastodons, so named because they used their long lower tusks as "shovels" to scoop up food.

Sloth: a small, slow-moving, now tree-living mammal. Some may live their entire life in just one tree. Large ground sloths are now extinct.

Species: all the individuals in a grouping of animals who are the same in every basic way; only members within a species can breed with one another and give birth to young like themselves.

Sport: another word meaning mutant.

Strontium: one of the more than 100 fundamental substances out of which all matter is made.

Survive: to keep on living (as an individual or species).

True elephant: any proboscidean having the later kind of teeth with rough ridges instead of teeth with raised cusps, as the mastodons did.

Tundra: flat treeless plain in cold Arctic and subarctic regions.

Vegetation: plant life.

Bibliography

Carrington, Richard. *Elephants: A Short Account of Their Natural History, Evolution and Influence on Mankind.* New York: Basic Books, 1959.

_____. *Mermaids and Mastodons.* New York: Rinehart and Co., 1957.

Colbert, Edwin H. *Evolution of the Vertebrates.* New York: John Wiley and Sons, 1955.

Kurten, Bjorn. *The Age of Mammals.* New York: Columbia University Press, 1979.

_____. *The Ice Age.* New York: G. P. Putnam's Sons, 1972.

_____. *Pleistocene Mammals of Europe.* Chicago: Aldine Publishing Co., 1968.

Loomis, Frederic Brewster. "Evolution of the Horse and Elephant." In *Creation by Evolution,* edited by Frances Mason. New York: Macmillan Co., 1928.

Lull, Richard S. "The Evolution of the Elephant." In Annual Report of Smithsonian Institute, 1908. Washington: Government Printing Office, 1909.

Maglio, Vincent J., and Cooke, H. B. S., eds. *Evolution of African Mammals.* Cambridge, MA: Harvard University Press, 1978.

Maglio, Vincent J. Translations of the American Philosophical Society, New Series, Volume 63, part 3, 1973.

Morewood-Dowsett, Joseph. "Elephant, Past and Present." Supplement to the *Journal of the Royal African Society*, Volume 38, No. 152. London: Macmillan and Co., July, 1939.

Osborn, Henry Fairfield. *Proboscidea.* Published by J. Pierpont Morgan Fund by the Trustees of the American Museum of Natural History. New York: The American Museum Press, 1936.

Scott, James. *Palaeontology.* New York: Taplinger Publishing Co., 1978.

Index

(Bold face indicates illustration)

Special Material

Author's Note, 60

Chart showing elephant's "family tree", 24–25

Map showing range of elephants past and present, 13

Time Chart, 1

A
Africa, 1, 7, 11, 12
 proboscideans in, 7, 11, 12, 22, 34, 36, 39, 41, 50, **52, 53, 54,** 55
African elephant, *see* elephant, African

Amebelodon, 21, **21**
American Museum of Natural History, 10, 17, 19
Anancus, 22, **22,** 45
Andrews, Charles 3, 10
Antarctica, 12
Armadillo (giant), 48, **49**
Asia
 proboscideans in, 1, 12–14, 17, 21, 22, 33, 41, 42, 45, 50, 53, **53,** 55
Asiatic elephant, *see* elephant, Asiatic
Australia, 12

B
Basilosaurus, **6,** 7, 60
Beadnell, Hugh, 3, 10
Beaver (giant), 48
Bering Strait, 12, 13, 17, 41
Big Bone Lick, Kentucky, 19

C
Cordillerion, 22, **23,** 39
Cuvier, Georges, 30

D
Deinotherium (or deinothere); also called "hoe-tusker"
 (possible) ancestors of, 15, 17; *see* chart pp. 24–25
 description, 14
 habitat and food, 15
 theories about, 14, 15
Desert, Sahara, 3, 7
Dugong, 57, 59
Dwarf elephant, 36, 37

E
Earth changes, 1, 11, 36, 37, 41, 45
Egypt, 3

Index

Elephant
   African, 50, **52**, 53, **54**, 55
   Asiatic (Indian), 50, 53, **53**, 55
   dangers to, 55
   dwarf, 36, 37
   ears, 52, 53
   feet and thighs 4, **5**, 7
   food, 47, 55
   habits, 55
   head, **2**, 50, 51, **51**
   Indian, *see* Asiatic elephant
   jaw, 17, 28, 50
   present day, 1, **2**, **5**, 50–55
   range today, 12, 13
   reproduction, 47
   size, 47, 53
   skull, **32**, 50
   teeth, 30, **31**, **32**, 50, 53
   "true elephants", 30, 33, 34, **35**, 36, 39
   trunk, 26, **27**, 28, 29, 55
Elephas falconeri, 36, 37
Elephas maximus, *see* elephant, Asiatic
Elephas namadicus, 36, 50, 60
Eocene, 1, 7, 11
Epochs, 1
Europe
   proboscideans in, 12–14, 17, 36, 41, 42, 45
Evolution, 28, 29
Extinctions, 45, 48, 49

F
Fayum, 7
fossils
   what we learn from them, 8

G
Genes, 29
Gnathabelodon, 21
Gomphothere, 1, 21–23, **20–23**, 24–25, 26, 28, 60
   (in) Ice Age, 41, 45
   (in) Pliocene **38**, 39
Ground Sloth (giant), 48, **49**

H
Hoe-tusker, *see Deinotherium*
Holocene, 1
Hunting (by Man), 48, 49
Hyrax, **56,** 57

I
Ice Age, 1, 41, 42, 45, 47–49
Imperial mammoth, **frontispiece**
Indian elephant, *see* elephant, Asiatic
Interglacial periods, 45

L
La Brea Tar Pits, **18,** 19
Lake Moeris, 7
Land bridge
   Africa to Europe, 12
   Bering Strait 12, 13, 17, 41
Long-jawed mastodon, *see* gomphothere
Loxodonta africana, *see* elephant, African

M
Malta, dwarf elephants of, 36, 37
Mammoth, 39, 45
   skeleton, 51, **51**
   Woolly, 39, **40,** 41, 42, **43,** 49

Man, 48, 49
Manatee, 57, **58,** 58
Map showing range of elephants, 15
Mastodon, **16,** 60
   contrasted with modern elephant, 17
   description, 17
   (in) Ice Age, 41, 45
   jaw and lip, 28
   long-jawed, *see* gomphothere
   skeleton, 51, **51**
   teeth, 30, **31**, 36
   true mastodon, 21
   trunk, 26
Miocene, 1, 34, 36, 37
Modern elephant, *see* elephant
Moeritherium, **1, 2,** 9
   appearance, general, 3
   discovery of, 3
   eyes and ears, 8
   extinction of, 11
   habitat and food, 7, 8
   legs and feet, 7
   skull, **4**
   teeth, **2**, 4
Mutant, mutation, 28, 29

N
Natural selection, 28, 37
North America, 1, 12, 17, 19, 21, 38, 39
   Ice Age in, 41, 42
   proboscideans in, 11–13, 17, 19, 21, 22, 36, 42, 48

O
Oligocene, 1, 8, 11
Osborn, Henry Fairfield, 10

P

Palaeoloxodon, 36, 60
Palaeomastodon, 1, **9**
    descendants, 23, 24–25
    description, 7
    extinction, 11
    habitat and food, 8
    when it lived, 8, 10
Philippine Islands, dwarf elephants on, 36
Phiomia, **1, 9, 10**
    descendants, 23, 24–25
    discovery and description, 7
    extinction, 11
    habitat and food, 7
    when it lived, 8, 10
Platybelodon, 21
Pleistocene, 1, 41, 42
Pliocene, 1, 34, **38**
Pre-elephants, 8
    jaw, 28
    (in) Pliocene, **38**, 39
    range, 12–13
    size and trunk, 26, 28
Present day elephants, *see* elephant
Proboscidea, proboscideans, 14
    number of species, 50

R

Rhynchotherium, 22

S

Sahara Desert, 3, 7
Santa Rosa Island, dwarf elephants on, 36
Sea cow, *see* dugong
Shovel-tusker, 21
South America
    proboscideans in, 12, 13, 23, 39, 41, 45
Species, *see Proboscidea*
"Sport", 29
Stegodon, 33, **33**, 34, 35
Stegotetrabelodon, 34, **35**, 36
Strontium, 8

T

Tethys Sea, 7
Time Chart, 1
Today's elephants, *see* elephant
Torynobelodon, 21
True mastodon, *see* mastodon

W

Warren mastodon, **16**, 17
Woolly mammoth, *see* mammoth
Woolly rhinoceros, **44**, 45

Z

Zeuglodon, see *Basilosaurus*